NUMBER PROPERTIES

Math Preparation Guide

This foundational guide provides a comprehensive analysis of the properties and rules of integers tested on the GMAT. Learn, practice, and master everything from prime products to perfect squares.

Number Properties GMAT Preparation Guide, 2007 Edition

10-digit International Standard Book Number: 0-9790175-0-5
13-digit International Standard Book Number: 978-0-9790175-0-6

Note: *GMAT, Graduate Management Admission Test, Graduate Management
Admission Council,* and *GMAC* are all registered trademarks of the Graduate
Management Admission Council which neither sponsors nor is affiliated in any way
with this product.

8 GUIDE INSTRUCTIONAL SERIES

Math GMAT Preparation Guides

Number Properties (ISBN: 978-0-9790175-0-6)

Fractions, Decimals, & Percents (ISBN: 978-0-9790175-1-3)

Equations, Inequalities, & VIC's (ISBN: 978-0-9790175-2-0)

Word Translations (ISBN: 978-0-9790175-3-7)

Geometry (ISBN: 978-0-9790175-4-4)

Verbal GMAT Preparation Guides

Critical Reasoning (ISBN: 978-0-9790175-5-1)

Reading Comprehension (ISBN: 978-0-9790175-6-8)

Sentence Correction (ISBN: 978-0-9790175-7-5)

HOW OUR GMAT PREP BOOKS ARE DIFFERENT

One of our core beliefs at Manhattan GMAT is that a curriculum should be more than just a guidebook of tricks and tips. Scoring well on the GMAT requires a curriculum that builds true content knowledge and understanding. Skim through this guide and this is what you will see:

You will *not* find page after page of guessing techniques.

Instead, you will find a highly organized and structured guide that actually teaches you the content you need to know to do well on the GMAT.

You *will* find many more pages-per-topic than in all-in-one tomes.

Each chapter covers one specific topic area in-depth, explaining key concepts, detailing in-depth strategies, and building specific skills through Manhattan GMAT's *In-Action* problem sets (with comprehensive explanations). Why are there 8 guides? Each of the 8 books (5 Math, 3 Verbal) covers a major content area in extensive depth, allowing you to delve into each topic in great detail. In addition, you may purchase only those guides that pertain to those areas in which you need to improve.

This guide is challenging - it asks you to do more, not less.

It starts with the fundamental skills, but does not end there; it also includes the *most advanced content* that many other prep books ignore. As the average GMAT score required to gain admission to top business schools continues to rise, this guide, together with the 6 computer adaptive online practice exams and bonus question bank included with your purchase, provides test-takers with the depth and volume of advanced material essential for achieving the highest scores, given the GMAT's computer adaptive format.

This guide is ambitious - developing mastery is its goal.

Developed by Manhattan GMAT's staff of REAL teachers (all of whom have 99th percentile official GMAT scores), our ambitious curriculum seeks to provide test-takers of all levels with an in-depth and carefully tailored approach that enables our students to achieve mastery. If you are looking to learn more than just the "process of elimination" and if you want to develop skills, strategies, and a confident approach to any problem that you may see on the GMAT, then our sophisticated preparation guides are the tools to get you there.

HOW TO ACCESS YOUR ONLINE RESOURCES

Please read this entire page of information, all the way down to the bottom of the page! This page describes WHAT online resources are included with the purchase of this book and HOW to access these resources.

[**If you are a registered Manhattan GMAT student** and have received this book as part of your course materials, you have AUTOMATIC access to ALL of our online resources. This includes all simulated practice exams, question banks, and online updates to this book. To access these resources, follow the instructions in the Welcome Guide provided to you at the start of your program. Do NOT follow the instructions below.]

If you have purchased this book, your purchase includes 1 YEAR OF ONLINE ACCESS to the following:

> **6 Computer Adaptive Online Practice Exams**

> **Bonus Online Question Bank for NUMBER PROPERTIES**

> **Online Updates to the Content in this Book**

The 6 full-length computer adaptive practice exams included with the purchase of this book are delivered online using Manhattan GMAT's proprietary computer adaptive online test engine. The exams adapt to your ability level by drawing from a bank of more than 1200 unique questions of varying difficulty levels written by Manhattan GMAT's expert instructors, all of whom have scored in the 99th percentile on the Official GMAT. At the end of each exam you will receive a score, an analysis of your results, and the opportunity to review detailed explanations for each question. You may choose to take the exams timed or untimed.

The Bonus Online Question Bank for Number Properties consists of 25 extra practice questions (with detailed explanations) that test the variety of Number Property concepts and skills covered in this book. These questions provide you with extra practice *beyond* the problem sets contained in this book. You may use our online timer to practice your pacing by setting time limits for each question in the bank.

The content presented in this book is updated periodically to ensure that it reflects the GMAT's most current trends. You may view all updates, including any known errors or changes, upon registering for online access.

Important Note: The 6 computer adaptive online exams included with the purchase of this book are the SAME exams that you receive upon purchasing ANY book in Manhattan GMAT's 8 Book Preparation Series. On the other hand, the Bonus Online Question Bank for NUMBER PROPERTIES is a unique resource that you receive ONLY with the purchase of this specific title.

To access the online resources listed above, you will need this book in front of you and you will need to register your information online. This book includes access to the above resources for ONE PERSON ONLY.

To register and start using your online resources, please go online to the following URL:

http://www.manhattangmat.com/access.cfm   (Double check that you have typed this in accurately!)

Your one-year of online access begins on the day that you register at the above URL. You only need to register your product ONCE at the above URL. To use your online resources any time AFTER you have completed the registration process, please login to the following URL:

http://www.manhattangmat.com/practicecenter.cfm

TABLE OF CONTENTS

g

Chapter 1
of
NUMBER PROPERTIES

DIVISIBILITY & PRIMES

In This Chapter . . .

INTEGERS

Integers are simply whole numbers such as 0, 1, 2, 3, etc. Integers can be positive (1, 2, 3, . .), negative (−1, −2, −3, . .), or the number 0.

The GMAT uses the term integer to mean a non-fraction or a non-decimal. The properties of integers form the basis of the Number Properties problem type.

Divisibility Rules

An integer is "divisible" by a number if the integer can be divided evenly by that number (meaning that there is no remainder). For example, 15 is divisible by 3 because it can be divided evenly by 3, but 15 is not divisible by 4. Alternatively, we can say that 3 is a divisor or a factor of 15. The Divisibility Rules are important shortcuts to determine whether an integer is divisible by 2, 3, 4, 5, 6, 8, 9, and 10. The GMAT frequently tests whether you have internalized these rules (especially on its more challenging questions), so it is important to memorize them.

An integer is divisible by:

2 if the integer is EVEN
12 is divisible by 2, but 13 is not.
3 if the SUM of the integer's DIGITS is divisible by 3
36 is divisible by 3 because the sum of its digits is 9, which is divisible by 3.
4 if the integer is divisible by 2 TWICE (if you can cut it in half twice)
28 is divisible by 4 because it is divisible by 2 once (=14) and again (=7).
5 if the integer ends in 0 or 5
75 and 80 are divisible by 5, but 77 and 83 are not.
6 if the integer is divisible by BOTH 2 and 3
48 is divisible by 6 since it is divisible by 2 (48 is even) AND by 3 (4 + 8 = 12).
8 if the integer is divisible by 2 THREE TIMES (if you can cut it in half 3 times)
32 is divisible by 8 since it is divisible by 2 once (16), twice (8), and a third time (4).
9 if the SUM of the integer's DIGITS is divisible by 9
4185 is divisible by 9 since the sum of its digits is 18, which is divisible by 9.
10 if the integer ends in 0
670 is divisible by 10, but 675 is not.

When you see a GMAT question with the word "remainder" in it, chances are that you are being asked to apply one of the divisibility rules.

Factors and Multiples

Factors and Multiples are essentially opposite terms.

A factor is a positive integer that divides evenly into an integer, so 1, 2, 4 and 8 are all the factors (also called divisors) of 8.

A multiple of an integer is formed by multiplying that integer by any whole number, so 8, 16, 24, and 32 are some of the multiples of 8.

Note that an integer is both a factor and a multiple of itself.

Fewer Factors, More Multiples

Sometimes it is easy to confuse factors and multiples. The mnemonic, "Fewer Factors, More Multiples," should help you remember the difference. Factors divide into an integer and are therefore less than or equal to that integer. Multiples, on the other hand, multiply out from an integer and are therefore greater than or equal to that integer.

There are a limited number of factors of a given integer; for example, there are only four factors of 8: 1, 2, 4, and 8. There are an infinite number of multiples of an integer; for example, the first 5 positive multiples of 8 are 8, 16, 24, 32, and 40, but one could go on listing multiples of 8 forever.

The Sum and the Difference Are Also Divisible

8 is a factor of 64, and 8 is also a factor of 40. Another way to put this: 64 is divisible by 8, and 40 is also divisible by 8. The sum of 64 and 40 (64 + 40 = 104) is also divisible by 8. Furthermore, the difference between 64 and 40 (64 − 40 = 24) is also divisible by 8.

Test it out (before you take the GMAT) and you will find that this rule always holds true: If 2 numbers have a common divisor, their SUM and DIFFERENCE retain that divisor as well.

Primes

A prime number is an integer (greater than 1) with exactly two factors: 1 and itself. In other words, a prime number has NO factors other than 1 and itself.

7 is prime because the only factors of 7 are 1 and 7.
8 is not prime because it is divisible by 2 and 4.

Note that the number 1 is not considered prime, as it has only one factor (itself). Therefore, the first prime number is 2, which is also the only even prime.

The first ten prime numbers are: 2, 3, 5, 7, 11, 13, 17, 19, 23, and 29. You should memorize these primes.

Prime Factorization

One very helpful way to analyze a number is to break it down into its prime factors. This can be done by creating a prime factor tree, as shown below with the number 72.

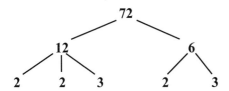

Prime factorization is extremely important on the GMAT because, once we know the prime factors of a number, we can determine ALL the factors of that number. ALL the factors of a number can be found by building all the products of the prime factors.

Factor Foundation Rule

Consider this rule that the GMAT expects you to know: If 72 is divisible by 12, then 72 is also divisible by all the factors of 12 (1, 2, 3, 4, 6, and 12). Written another way, if 12 is a factor of 72, then all the factors of 12 are also factors of 72. We call this the Factor Foundation Rule because it allows us to conceive of factors as building blocks that are the foundation upon which numbers are built. 12 and 6 are factors, or building blocks, of 72 (because 12×6 builds 72). But 12, in turn, is built from its own factors; for example, 4×3 builds 12. Thus, if 72 rests partially on the foundation of its factor 12, but 12 in turn rests on the foundation built by its prime factors 2, 2, and 3, then 72 is also built on the foundation of 2, 2, and 3.

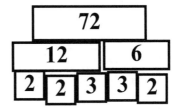

Note that the number 1 is a non-prime factor of all integers. Remember to include 1 when counting the factors of any number.

The Prime Box

The easiest way to work with the Factor Foundation Rule is with a tool called a Prime Box. A Prime Box is exactly what its name implies: a box that holds all the prime factors of a number. Here are prime boxes for 72, 12, and 125:

72	12	125
2, 2, 2, 3, 3	2, 2, 3	5, 5, 5

The factors of 72 can be generated by (1) finding the prime factors of 72, and then (2) creating all the possible prime products.

$2 \times 2 = 4$ $2 \times 2 \times 2 = 8$ $2 \times 2 \times 2 \times 3 = 24$
$2 \times 3 = 6$ $2 \times 2 \times 3 = 12$ $2 \times 2 \times 3 \times 3 = 36$
$3 \times 3 = 9$ $2 \times 3 \times 3 = 18$ $2 \times 2 \times 2 \times 3 \times 3 = 72$

Don't forget that 2 and 3 themselves are factors -- and 1 is always a factor too!

The GMAT's Prime Product Obsession

You can use the prime box to test whether or not a specific number is a factor of another number.

Is 27 a factor of 72?

72

$$2, 2, 2, \\ 3, 3$$

$27 = 3 \times 3 \times 3$. We cannot make 27 from the prime factors of 72. Therefore, 27 is not a factor of 72.

> Prime boxes can help you solve problems about divisibility as well as GCF and LCM.

Given that the integer *n* is divisible by 3, 7, and 11, what other numbers must be divisors of *n*?

n

$$3, 7, 11$$

Since we know that 3, 7, and 11 are prime factors of *n*, we know that *n* must also be divisible by all the possible prime products: 21, 33, 77, and 231.

Without even knowing what *n* is, we have found 4 more of its factors: 21, 33, 77, and 231.

Greatest Common Factor and Least Common Multiple

Greatest Common Factor: the largest number by which two integers can be divided.
Least Common Multiple: the smallest number that is a multiple of two integers.

You can use prime boxes to find the GCF and LCM of two integers.

What are the GCF and LCM of 30 and 24?

30

$$2, 3, 5$$

24

$$2, 2, 2, \\ 3$$

If a number appears more than once, use the following guidelines:
    GCF: Use the lower power.
    LCM: Use the higher power.

To find the GCF, find the product of the **common** prime factors, using the lower power of the repeated factor (2^1 instead of 2^3): $2 \times 3 = 6$.

To find the LCM, find the product of **all** the prime factors of both numbers, using the higher power of the repeated factor (2^3 instead of 2^1): $2 \times 2 \times 2 \times 3 \times 5 = 120$.

Problem Set

For problems #1-11, use one or more prime boxes to answer each question: YES, NO, or CANNOT BE DETERMINED. If your answer is CANNOT BE DETERMINED, use two numerical examples to show how the problem could go either way.

1. If a is divided by 7 and by 18, an integer results. Is $\dfrac{a}{42}$ an integer?

2. If 80 is a factor of r, is 15 a factor of r?

3. Given that 7 is a factor of n and 7 is a factor of p, is $n + p$ divisible by 7?

4. Given that 8 is not a factor of g, is 8 a factor of $2g$?

5. If j is divisible by 12 and 10, is j divisible by 24?

6. If 12 is a factor of xyz, is 12 a factor of xy?

7. Given that 6 is a divisor of r and r is a factor of s, is 6 a factor of s?

8. If 24 is a factor of h and 28 is a factor of k, must 21 be a factor of hk?

9. If 6 is not a factor of d, is $12d$ divisible by 6?

10. If k is divisible by 6 and $3k$ is not divisible by 5, is k divisible by 10?

11. If 60 is a factor of u, is 18 a factor of u?

Solve the following problems.

12. What is the greatest common factor of 420 and 660?

13. What is the least common multiple of 18 and 24?

14. If w is a prime number, and $z = 36w$, what is the least common multiple of z and $6w$, in terms of w?

15. If $y = 30p$, and p is prime, what is the greatest common factor of y and $14p$, in terms of p?

1. YES:

a

2, 3, 3, 7

If a is divisible by 7 and by 18, its prime factors include 2, 3, 3, and 7, as indicated by the prime box to the left. Therefore, any integer that can be constructed as a product of any of these prime factors is also a factor of a. $42 = 2 \times 3 \times 7$. Therefore, 42 is also a factor of a.

2. CANNOT BE DETERMINED:

r

2, 2, 2, 2, 5

If r is divisible by 80, its prime factors include 2, 2, 2, 2, and 5, as indicated by the prime box to the left. Therefore, any integer that can be constructed as a product of any of these prime factors is also a factor of r. $15 = 3 \times 5$. Since the prime factor 3 is not in the prime box, we cannot determine whether or not 15 is a factor of r. Remember, this prime box represents a partial listing of the prime factors of r. There could be additional prime factors.

3. **YES:** If 2 numbers have a common divisor, their SUM retains that divisor too. Since n and p share the common factor, 7, the sum of n and p must also be divisible by 7.

4. CANNOT BE DETERMINED:

2g

2, g

In order for 8 to be a factor of $2g$, we would need two more 2's in the prime box. By the Factor Foundation Rule, g would need to be divisible by 4. We know that g is not divisible by 8, but there are certainly integers that are divisible by 4 and not by 8: 4, 12, 20, 28, etc... However, while we cannot conclude that g is **not** divisible by 4, we cannot be certain that g **is** divisible by 4 either.

5. CANNOT BE DETERMINED:

j

2, 2, 3, 5

If j is divisible by 12 and by 10, its prime factors include 2, 2, 3, and 5, as indicated by the prime box to the left. Therefore, any integer that can be constructed as a product of any of these prime factors is also a factor of j. $24 = 2 \times 2 \times 2 \times 3$. There are only two 2's in the prime box; therefore, 24 is not necessarily a factor of j.

6. CANNOT BE DETERMINED:

xyz

2, 2, 3

If xyz is divisible by 12, its prime factors include 2, 2, and 3, as indicated by the prime box to the left. Those prime factors could all be factors of x and y, in which case 12 is a factor of xy. This is the case when $x = 20$, $y = 3$, and $z = 7$. However, x and y could be prime or otherwise not divisible by 2, 2, and 3, in which case xy is not divisible by 12. This is the case when $x = 5$, $y = 11$, and $z = 24$.

7. **YES:** By the Factor Foundation Rule, if 6 is a factor of *r* and *r* is a factor of *s*, then 6 is a factor of *s*.

8. **YES:**

hk

h	*k*
2, 2,	2, 2,
2, 3	7

By the Factor Foundation Rule, all the factors of both *h* and *k* must be factors of the product, *hk*. Therefore, the factors of *hk* include 2, 2, 2, 2, 2, 3, and 7, as shown in the prime box to the left. $21 = 3 \times 7$. 3 and 7 are both in the prime box. Therefore, 21 is a factor of *hk*.

9. **YES:**

12d

12	*d*
2, 2,	not 2
3	not 3

The fact that *d* is not divisible by 6 is irrelevant in this case. Since 12 is divisible by 6, 12*d* is also divisible by 6.

10. **NO:**

3k

3	*k*
3	2, 3
	not 5

We know that 3*k* is not divisible by 5. Since 5 is prime, and 3 is not divisible by 5, we can conclude that *k* is not divisible by 5. If *k* is not divisible by 5, it cannot be divisible by 10.

11. **CANNOT BE DETERMINED:**

u

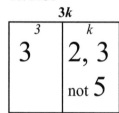

If *u* is divisible by 60, its prime factors include 2, 2, 3, and 5, as indicated by the prime box to the left. Therefore, any integer that can be constructed as a product of any of these prime factors is also a factor of *u*. $18 = 2 \times 3 \times 3$. Since there is only one 3 in the prime box, we cannot determine whether or not 18 is a factor of *u*. Remember, this prime box represents a partial listing of the prime factors of *u*. There could be additional prime factors.

12. **60:**

420

| 2, 2, 3, |
| 5, 7 |

660

| 2, 2, 3, |
| 5, 11 |

The greatest common factor of 420 and 660 is the product of all the shared factors: $2 \times 2 \times 3 \times 5 = 60$.

13. **72:**

18	24
2, 3, 3	2, 2, 2, 3

The least common multiple of 18 and 24 is the product of all the factors of both integers, using the higher power of repeated factors: (2^3 instead of 2^1 and 3^2 instead of 3^1).
$2 \times 2 \times 2 \times 3 \times 3 = 72$.

14. **36w:**

z (36w)	6w
2, 2, 3, 3, w	2, 3, w

The least common multiple of z and $6w$ is the product of all the factors of both integers, using the higher power of repeated factors: (2^2 instead of 2^1 and 3^2 instead of 3^1).
$2 \times 2 \times 3 \times 3 \times w = 36w$.

15. **2p:**

y (30p)	14p
2, 3, 5, p	2, 7, p

The greatest common factor of y and $15p$ is the product of all the common prime factors, using the lower power of repeated factors: $2 \times p = 2p$.

Chapter 2
of
NUMBER PROPERTIES

ODDS & EVENS

In This Chapter . . .

ODDS & EVENS

Simply put, even numbers are divisible by 2, while odd numbers are not.

Evens: 0, 2, 4, 6, 8, 10, 12, . . .

Odds: 1, 3, 5, 7, 9, 11, . . .

The GMAT tests your knowledge of how odd and even numbers combine through addition, subtraction, multiplication, and division.

Odd (and Even) Poetry

Rules for adding, subtracting, multiplying and dividing odd and even numbers can be derived by simply picking numbers and testing them out. For example, pick two odd numbers (9 and 17) and see what happens when you add them up: you get an even number (26). You can then generalize that whenever you add two odd numbers, you will get an even number. While this is certainly a valid strategy, it also pays to memorize and internalize the following two rules for operating with odds and evens, as they are extremely useful for certain GMAT math questions.

If you forget these rules, you can always figure them out on the test by picking real numbers.

Addition and Subtraction:
Add 2 odds or add 2 evens and EVEN you shall see $7 + 11 = 18$ and $8 + 6 = 14$
But add an odd with an even and oh how ODD t'will be. $7 + 8 = 15$

Note that the same rule holds true for subtraction.

Multiplication:
Just one EVEN number in a multiplication set $3 \times \mathbf{8} \times 9 \times 13 = 2808$
And no matter all the others, an EVEN you will get.

Note that the converse is true as well: if there is no even number in a multiplication set, then an odd number you will get.

Division:
There are no guaranteed outcomes in division because the division of two integers may not yield an integer result (if the numerator is smaller than the denominator).

The Sum of Two Primes

Notice that all prime numbers are odd, except the number 2. (All subsequent even numbers are, by definition, divisible by 2, so there is no way they could be prime.) As such, the sum of any two primes will be even ("Add two odds . . ."), unless one of those primes is the number 2. So, if you see a sum of two primes that is odd, one of those primes must be the number 2.

Problem Set

Answer each question ODD, EVEN, or CANNOT BE DETERMINED. Try to explain each answer using the rules you learned in this section.

1.   If n is odd, p is even, and q is odd, what is $n + p + q$?

2.   If r is a prime number greater than 2, and s is odd, what is rs?

3.   If t is odd, what is t^4?

4.   If u is even and w is odd, what is $u + uw$?

5.   If $x \div y$ yields an odd integer, what is x?

6.   If $a + b$ is even, what is ab?

7.   If c, d, and e are consecutive integers, what is cde?

8.   If f and g are prime numbers, what is $f + g$?

9.   If h is even, j is odd, and k is odd, what is $k(h + j)$?

10.   If m is odd, what is $m^2 + m$?

11.   If n, p, q, and r are consecutive integers, what is their sum?

12.   If s is even and $t = s - 3$, what is $s + t$?

13.   If u is odd and w is even, what is $(uw)^2 + u$?

14.   If xy is even and z is even, what is $x + z$?

15.   If a, b, and c are consecutive integers, what is $a + b + c$?

1. **EVEN:** O + E = O. O + O = E. If in doubt, try plugging in actual numbers: 7 + 2 + 3 = 12 (even).

2. **ODD:** O $\times$ O = O. If in doubt, try plugging in actual numbers: 3 $\times$ 5 = 15 (odd).

3. **ODD:** O $\times$ O $\times$ O $\times$ O = O. If in doubt, try plugging in actual numbers: 3 $\times$ 3 $\times$ 3 $\times$ 3 = 81 (odd).

4. **EVEN:** uw is even. (Just one even in a multiplication set, and an even you will get.) E + E = E.

5. **CANNOT BE DETERMINED:** There are no guaranteed outcomes in division.

6. **CANNOT BE DETERMINED:** If $a + b$ is even, a and b are either both odd or both even. If they are both odd, ab is odd. If they are both even, ab is even.

7. **EVEN:** At least one of the consecutive integers, c, d, and e, must be even. Therefore, the product, cde, must be even. (Just one even in a multiplication set, and an even you will get.)

8. **CANNOT BE DETERMINED:** If either f or g is 2, $f + g$ will be odd. If f and g are odd primes, $f + g$ will be even.

9. **ODD:** $h + j$ must be odd (E + O = O). Therefore, $k(h + j)$ must be odd (O $\times$ O = O).

10. **EVEN:** m^2 must be odd (O $\times$ O = O). $m^2 + m$, therefore, must be even (O + O = E).

11. **EVEN:** If n, p, q, and r are consecutive integers, two of them must be odd and two of them must be even. You can pair them up to add them: O + O = E, and E + E = E. Adding the pairs, you will see that the sum must be even: E + E = E.

12. **ODD:** If s is even, then t must be odd. (Try plugging in real numbers: if $s = 2$, $t = 5$.) E + O = O.

13. **ODD:** $(uw)^2$ must be even. (Just one even in a multiplication set, and an even number you will get.) E + O = O.

14. **CANNOT BE DETERMINED:** If xy is even, then either x or y (or both x and y) must be even. Given that z is even, $x + z$ could be O + E or E + E. Therefore, we cannot determine whether $x + z$ is odd or even.

15. **CANNOT BE DETERMINED:** If a, b, and c are consecutive, then there could be either one or two even integers in the set. $a + b + c$ could be O + E + O or E + O + E. In the first case, the sum is even; in the second, the sum is odd.

Chapter 3
of
NUMBER PROPERTIES

POSITIVES & NEGATIVES

In This Chapter . . .

- Absolute Value: Absolutely Positive
- A Double Negative = A Positive
- Multiplying & Dividing Signed Numbers
- Systematic Testing

POSITIVES & NEGATIVES

Numbers can be either positive or negative (except the number 0, which is neither). Positives and negatives can be easily understood by considering temperature. If we say that it is 5 degrees outside, we mean that it is 5 degrees above 0 (a positive number). If we say that it is -5 degrees, we mean that it is 5 degrees below 0 (a negative number).

A number line illustrates this idea:

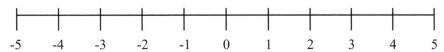

Negative numbers are all to the left of zero. Positive numbers are all to the right of zero.

Note that a variable (such as x) can have either a positive or negative value, in general. The variable x is not necessarily positive; nor is $-x$ necessarily negative.

Absolute Value: Absolutely Positive

The absolute value of a number answers this question: How far away is the number from 0 on the number line? For example, the number 5 is exactly 5 units away from 0, so the absolute value of 5 equals 5. Mathematically, we write this using the symbol for absolute value: $|5| = 5$. To find the absolute value of -5, look at the number line above: -5 is also exactly 5 units away from 0. Thus, the absolute value of -5 equals 5, or, in mathematical symbols, $|-5| = 5$. Notice that absolute value is always positive, because it disregards the direction (positive or negative) from which the number approaches 0 on the number line. When you interpret a number in an absolute value sign, just think: Absolutely Positive! (Except, of course, for 0, because $|0| = 0$.)

A Double Negative = A Positive

A double negative occurs when a minus sign is in front of a negative number (which already has its own negative sign). For example:

What is $7 - (-3)$?

Just as you learned in English class, two negatives yield a positive:

$7 - (-3) = 7 + 3 = 10.$

The absolute value of any non-zero number is always positive.

Multiplying & Dividing Signed Numbers

When you multiply two numbers, positive or negative, follow one simple rule:

If **S**igns are the **S**ame, the answer's po**S**itive $7 \times 8 = 56$ & $(-7) \times (-8) = 56$
but if **N**ot, the answer is **N**egative. $(-7) \times 8 = -56$ & $7 \times (-8) = -56$

The same rule applies for division. $56 \div 7 = 8$ & $-56 \div (-8) = 7$
$56 \div (-7) = -8$ & $-56 \div 8 = -7$

Systematic Testing

On the GMAT, you may see problems that deal with positives and negatives, in which you are asked to evaluate the signs of variable expressions. For example:

If $ab > 0$, which of the following must be negative?

(A) $a + b$ (B) $|a| + b$ (C) $b - a$

(D) $\dfrac{a}{b}$ (E) $-\dfrac{a}{b}$

One way to solve problems like this is to systematically test numbers. Use a chart such as the one shown below to keep track of your work. First, test each of the four possible positive/negative combinations to see if they meet the criteria established in the question stem. Eliminate any that do not meet these criteria. Then test each of the remaining combinations in each of the answer choices. If more than one answer choice gives you the desired result for all cases, try another pair of numbers and test those answer choices again.

	Question	A	B	C	D	E
	$ab > 0$	$a + b$	$|a| + b$	$b - a$	$\dfrac{a}{b}$	$-\dfrac{a}{b}$
$+, +$ $a = 3$ $b = 6$	YES	POS	POS	POS	POS	NEG
$-, +$ $a = -3$ $b = 6$	NO					
$-, -$ $a = -3$ $b = -6$	YES	NEG	NEG	NEG	POS	NEG
$+, -$ $a = 3$ $b = -6$	NO					

When multiplying and dividing signed numbers, follow the Same Sign Rule.

Problem Set

Solve problems #1-5. Pay careful attention to absolute value signs.

1. $\dfrac{-208}{-4}$

2. $66 \div (-33) \times \left| -9 \right|$

3. $\dfrac{-30}{-5} \div \left| 8 \right|$

4. $(-6)\left| 2 \times (-5) \right|$

5. $\dfrac{20 \times (-7)}{-35 \times (-2)}$

In problems #6-15, decide whether the expression described is POSITIVE, NEGATIVE, or CANNOT BE DETERMINED. If you answer CANNOT BE DETERMINED, give numerical examples to show how the problem could go either way.

6. The product of 3 negative numbers

7. The quotient of one negative and one positive number

8. xy, given that $x < 0$ and $y \neq 0$

9. $\left| x \right| \times y^2$, given that $xy \neq 0$

10. $\dfrac{x}{y} \div z$, given that x, y, and z are negative

11. $\dfrac{\left| ab \right|}{b}$, given that $b < a < 0$

12. $-4\left| d \right|$, given that $d \neq 0$

13. $\dfrac{rst}{w}$, given that $r < s < 0 < w < t$

14. $h^4 k^3 m^2$, given that $k < 0$, $h \neq 0$, and $m \neq 0$

15. $\dfrac{-x}{(-y)(-z)}$, given that $xyz > 0$

1. **52:** In division, use the Same Sign rule. In this case, the signs are the same; therefore, the answer is positive.

2. **−18:** In division, use the Same Sign rule. In this case, the signs are not the same; therefore, the answer is negative. Then, multiply by the absolute value of −9, which is 9. To multiply −2 × 9, use the Same Sign rule: the signs are not the same, so the answer is negative.

3. **3/4:** This is a two-step multiplication problem. Use the Same Sign rule for both steps. In the first step, the signs are the same; therefore, the answer is positive. In the second step, the signs are again the same. The final answer is positive.

4. **−60:** This is really a single-step problem, even though it may look like two. The signs of the numbers within the absolute value symbols are not important. The sign of the product must be positive, according to the definition of absolute value. Therefore, the problem is simply a negative integer multiplied by a positive integer, and the answer must be negative.

5. **−2:** The sign of the first product, 20 × (−7), is negative (by the Same Sign rule). The sign of the second product, −35 × (−2), is positive (by the Same Sign rule). Applying the Same Sign rule to the final division problem, the final answer must be negative.

6. **NEGATIVE:** Do this problem in two steps. The product of the first two negative numbers will be positive. A positive number times a negative number will be negative.

7. **NEGATIVE:** By the Same Sign rule, the quotient of one negative and one positive number must be negative.

8. **CANNOT BE DETERMINED:** x is negative; however, y could be either positive or negative. Therefore, we have no way to determine whether the product, xy, is positive or negative.

9. **POSITIVE:** $|x|$ and y^2 will both be positive, the first because of the definition of absolute value, and the second because y^2 will be either positive × positive or negative × negative. The product of two positive numbers is positive, by the Same Sign rule.

10. **NEGATIVE:** Do this problem in two steps: First, a negative number divided by a negative number yields a positive number (by the Same Sign rule). Second, a positive number divided by a negative number yields a negative number (again, by the Same Sign rule).

11. **NEGATIVE:** a and b are both negative numbers. Therefore, this problem is a positive number (by the definition of absolute value) divided by a negative number. By the Same Sign rule, the answer will be negative.

12. **NEGATIVE:** You do not need to know the sign of d to solve this problem. Because it is within the absolute value symbols, you can treat it as a positive number. By the Same Sign rule, a negative number times a positive number yields a negative number.

13. **POSITIVE:** r and s are negative; w and t are positive. Therefore, rst is a positive number. A positive number divided by another positive number yields a positive number.

14. **NEGATIVE:** Integers raised to even exponents always yield positive numbers. Therefore, h^4 and m^2 are both positive. Because k is negative, k^3 is negative. Therefore, the final product, $h^4k^3m^2$, is the product of two positives and a negative, which is negative.

15. **NEGATIVE:** Simplifying the original fraction yields: $\dfrac{-x}{yz}$.

If the product xyz is positive, then there are two possible scenarios: (1) all the integers are positive, or (2) two of the integers are negative and the third is positive. Test out both scenarios, using real numbers. In the first case, the end result is negative. In the second case, the two negative integers will essentially cancel each other out. Again, the end result is negative. Try both cases out with real numbers if you have any doubts about this.

Chapter 4
of
NUMBER PROPERTIES

CONSECUTIVE INTEGERS

In This Chapter . . .

- Be Inclusive and Add One Before You're Done
- The Sum of Consecutive Integers
- The Average Term in a Consecutive Set
- Special Products
- Special Sums
- Consecutive Integers and Divisibility

CONSECUTIVE INTEGERS

Consecutive numbers are numbers that follow immediately, one after another, without skipping, from a given starting point. For example, 4, 5, 6, 7 are consecutive integers, but 4, 6, 7, 9 are not. There are many other types of consecutive patterns, as exemplified below:

Consecutive Even Integers: 8, 10, 12, 14 (8, 10, 14, 16 is incorrect, as it skips 12)

Consecutive Primes: 11, 13, 17, 19 (11, 13, 15, 17 is wrong, as 15 is not prime)

Be Inclusive and Add One Before You're Done

How many integers are there from 6 to 10? Four, right? Wrong! There are actually five integers from 6 to 10! Count them and you'll see: 6, 7, 8, 9, 10. It is easy to forget that you have to include (or, in GMAT lingo, **be inclusive of**) extremes. In this case, both extremes (the numbers 6 and 10) must be counted; when you merely subtract ($10 - 6 = 4$), you are forgetting to include the first extreme (6), as it has been subtracted away (along with 5, 4, 3, 2, and 1).

Does this mean that you must methodically count each term in a long consecutive pattern? No, just remember that if both extremes should be counted, you need to add 1 before you're done.

How many integers are there from 14 to 765, inclusive?

$765 - 14$, plus 1, yields 752.

Sometimes, however, it is just easier to list the terms of a consecutive pattern and count them (especially when one or both of the extremes are not included).

How many multiples of 7 are there from 8 to 49, inclusive?

List them: 14, 21, 28, 35, 42, 49. Count the number of terms to get the answer: Six.

Use these shortcuts on consecutive integer problems to save time on the test.

The Sum of Consecutive Integers

Consider the problem below:

What is the sum of all the integers from 20 to 100, inclusive?

Adding all those integers would take much longer than you have for a GMAT problem. Here's the shortcut:

(1)   Average the first and last term to find the precise "middle" of the set: $100 + 20 = 120$ and $120 \div 2 = 60$.
(2)   Count the number of terms: $100 - 20 = 80$, plus 1 yields 81.
(3)   Multiply the "middle" number by the number of terms to find the sum: $60 \times 81 = 4,860$

> Think of the average term of a consecutive set as the number that lies precisely in the middle of that set.

The Average Term in a Consecutive Set

Consider this problem:

What is the average of all the integers from 20 to 100, inclusive?

If you know the FIRST and LAST terms of the set, simply find the middle number:

$$100 + 20 = 120 \text{ and } 120 \div 2 = 60$$

If you only know the SUM of the set and the # OF TERMS in the set, use the average formula:

$$\frac{\text{sum of all integers}}{\text{\# of integers}} = \frac{4860}{81} = 60$$

Note these important facts:
The average of an odd number of consecutive integers (1, 2, 3, 4, 5) will always be an integer (3).
On the other hand, the average of an even number of consecutive integers (1, 2, 3, 4) will never be an integer (2.5), because there is no true middle number.

Special Products

Can you come up with a series of 3 consecutive integers in which none of the integers is a multiple of 3? Go ahead, try it!

You will quickly see that any set of 3 consecutive integers must contain one multiple of 3. The result is that the product of any set of 3 consecutive integers is divisible by 3.

$1 \times 2 \times 3 = 6$	$4 \times 5 \times 6 = 120$	**Notice that all of these products**
$2 \times 3 \times 4 = 24$	$5 \times 6 \times 7 = 210$	**are divisible by 3!**
$3 \times 4 \times 5 = 60$	$6 \times 7 \times 8 = 336$	

According to the Factor Foundation Rule, every number is divisible by all the factors of its factors. If there is always a multiple of 3 in a set of 3 consecutive integers, the product of the integers will always be divisible by 3.

The same logic applies to a set of 4 consecutive integers, 5 consecutive integers, and every other number of consecutive integers. The product of any set of 4 consecutive integers will be divisible by 4; the product of any set of 5 consecutive integers will be divisible by 5.

This rule applies to any number of consecutive integers.

Special Sums

Find the sum of any 3 consecutive terms:

$1 + 2 + 3 = 6$	Notice that both sums are multiples of 3.
$8 + 9 + 10 = 27$	(Or, both sums are divisible by 3.)

Find the sum of any 5 consecutive terms:

$4 + 5 + 6 + 7 + 8 = 30$	Notice that both sums are multiples of 5.
$13 + 14 + 15 + 16 + 17 = 75$	(Or, both sums are divisible by 5.)

For any set of consecutive integers with an odd number of terms, the sum of all the integers is always a multiple of the # of terms. Note that this rule does NOT work for the sum of a consecutive set with an even number of terms.

Find the sum of any 4 consecutive terms:

$1 + 2 + 3 + 4 = 10$	Notice that NEITHER sum is a multiple of 4.
$8 + 9 + 10 + 11 = 38$	

This rule only applies to a set of consecutive integers with an *odd* number of terms.

Note that the special sums rule only works for a set of consecutive integers with an odd number of terms.

Why does this work? Consider any set of consecutive integers: n, $n + 1$, $n + 2$, $n + 3$, etc...

The sum of the first three integers is $n + n{+}1 + n{+}2$, or $3n + 3$. This is divisible by 3. However, the sum of the first four integers is $n + n{+}1 + n{+}2 + n{+}3$, or $4n + 6$. This is not divisible by 4. You can extend this algebraic explanation to see that the rule will apply only to a set of consecutive integers with an odd number of terms.

Consecutive Integers and Divisibility

If there is one even integer in a consecutive series, the product of the series is divisible by 2. If there are two even integers in a consecutive series, the product of the series is divisible by 4. We can use a prime box to illustrate this rule:

If x and $x + 2$ are even, 2 is a factor of $x(x + 1)(x + 2)$ twice. Therefore, the prime product $2 \times 2 = 4$ is a factor of the product of the series.

x	$x + 1$	$x + 2$
2		2

Consider this example:

If $x^3 - x = p$, and x is even, is p divisible by 4?

If we factor x out of the expression $x^3 - x$, we get $x(x^2 - 1)$. If we further factor this expression, we get $x(x + 1)(x - 1)$. This is a product of consecutive integers $(x - 1)x(x + 1)$. Therefore, we have the product of two odd integers and one even. Constructing a prime box shows that 4 is not necessarily a factor of p.

$(x - 1)$	x	$(x + 1)$
	2	

Problem Set

Solve these problems using the rules for consecutive integers.

1.   How many primes are there from 10 to 41, inclusive?

2.   If x, y, and z are consecutive integers, is $x + y + z$ divisible by 3?

3.   What is the sum of all the positive integers to 100, inclusive?

4.   Will the average of 6 consecutive integers be an integer?

5.   In a sequence of 8 consecutive integers, how much greater is the sum of the last four integers than the sum of the first four integers?

6.   If the sum of a set of 10 consecutive integers is 195, what is the average of the set?

7.   How many terms are there in the set of consecutive integers from -18 to 33, inclusive?

8.   Find the sum of 5 consecutive integers whose average is 50.

9.   If r, s, and t are consecutive positive multiples of 3, is rst divisible by 27, 54, or both?

10.   Is the sum of the integers from 54 to 153, inclusive, divisible by 100?

11.   List six factors of the product of 5 consecutive even integers.

12.   If the sum of the last 3 integers in a set of 6 consecutive integers is 624, what is the sum of the first 3 integers of the set?

13.   What is the average of 11 consecutive integers whose sum is -286?

14.   If a, b, c, and d are consecutive integers, is $d + a > b + c$?

15.   If the sum of the last 3 integers in a set of 7 consecutive integers is 258, what is the sum of the first 4 integers?

1. **9:** The primes from 10 to 41, inclusive, are: 11, 13, 17, 19, 23, 29, 31, 37, and 41.

2. **YES:** For any odd number of terms, the sum of a consecutive set of integers is divisible by the number of integers in the set. (See the section on Special Sums and Products.)

3. **5,050:** There are 100 integers from 1 to 100, inclusive: $(100 - 1) + 1$. (Remember to add one before you're done.) The number exactly in the middle is 50.5. (You can find the middle term by averaging the first and last terms of the set.) Therefore, multiply 100 by 50.5 to find the sum of all the integers in the set: $100 \times 50.5 = 5,050$.

4. **NO:** In order for the average of 6 integers to be an integer, the sum of the integers must be divisible by 6. The special sums rule does not hold true for a set with an even number of terms, as illustrated by the following example:
$$\frac{4 + 5 + 6 + 7 + 8 + 9}{6} = \frac{39}{6} = 6.5$$

5. **16:** Think of the set of integers as n, $(n + 1)$, $(n + 2)$, $(n + 3)$, $(n + 4)$, $(n + 5)$, $(n + 6)$, and $(n + 7)$.
First find the sum of the first 4 integers:
$$n + (n + 1) + (n + 2) + (n + 3) = 4n + 6$$
Then find the sum of the next 4 integers:
$$(n + 4) + (n + 5) + (n + 6) + (n + 7) = 4n + 22$$
The difference between these two partial sums is:
$$(4n + 22) - (4n + 6) = 22 - 6 = 16$$

6. **19.5:** $\text{Average} = \dfrac{\text{Sum}}{\text{\# of terms}} : \dfrac{195}{10} = 19.5$. The fact that the integers are consecutive is not important.

7. **52:** $33 - (-18) = 51$. Then add one before you're done: 52.

8. **250:** Sum = Average $\times$ # of terms: $50 \times 5 = 250$. The fact that the integers are consecutive is not important.

9. **BOTH:** By the Factor Foundation Rule, the product of three consecutive multiples of 3 must have, as factors, all the factors of those integers. 3 is a factor of each of the integers. Therefore, the product rst must have three 3's as factors. Additionally, at least one of the integers must be even, so the product will have a 2 as a factor. $27 = 3 \times 3 \times 3$ can be constructed from the known prime factors and is therefore a factor of the product rst. $54 = 2 \times 3 \times 3 \times 3$ can also be constructed from the known prime factors and therefore is another factor of the product rst.

r	s	t
3	3	3
	2	

10. **NO:** There are 100 integers from 54 to 153, inclusive. The special sums rule does not hold true for a set with an even number of terms.

11. **1, 2, 4, 8, 16, and 32:** By the Factor Foundation Rule, the product of five consecutive even integers (a, b, c, d, and e) must have, as factors, all the factors of those even integers. 2 is a factor of every even integer. Therefore, the product must have five 2's as factors. The five numbers listed above can be constructed as products of one or more of those 2's.

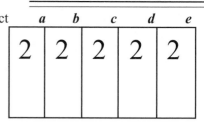

$$2 \times 2 = \mathbf{4} \qquad 2 \times 2 \times 2 = \mathbf{8} \qquad 2 \times 2 \times 2 \times 2 = \mathbf{16} \qquad 2 \times 2 \times 2 \times 2 \times 2 = \mathbf{32}$$

Finally, remember to include 1 in your list, since 1 is a factor of every integer.

12. **615:** Think of the set of integers as n, $(n + 1)$, $(n + 2)$, $(n + 3)$, $(n + 4)$, and $(n + 5)$. $(n + 3) + (n + 4) + (n + 5) = 3n + 12 = 624$. Therefore, $n = 204$. The sum of the first three integers, $204 + 205 + 206 = 615$.

Alternately: the sum of the first three integers is $3n + 3$. If $3n + 12 = 624$, $3n = 612$.
      Therefore, $3n + 3 = 615$.

13. **−26:** Average $= \dfrac{\text{Sum}}{\text{\# of terms}} : \dfrac{-286}{11} = -26$

14. **NO:** Think of the set of integers a, b, c, and d as n, $(n + 1)$, $(n + 2)$, and $(n + 3)$. Substituting these expressions into the inequality, you get: "Is $(n + 3) + n > (n + 1) + (n + 2)$?" This can be simplified: "Is $2n + 3 > 2n + 3$?" These expressions are equal; neither is greater than the other.

15. **330:** Think of the set of integers as n, $(n + 1)$, $(n + 2)$, $(n + 3)$, $(n + 4)$, $(n + 5)$, and $(n + 6)$. $(n + 4) + (n + 5) + (n + 6) = 3n + 15 = 258$. Therefore, $n = 81$. The sum of the first four integers, $81 + 82 + 83 + 84 = 330$.

Alternately: the sum of the first four integers is $4n + 6$. If $n = 81$, then $4n + 6 = 4(81) + 6 = 330$.

*Manhattan*GMAT*Prep
the new standard

g

Chapter 5
of
NUMBER PROPERTIES

EXPONENTS

In This Chapter . . .

- Wow, That Increased Exponentially!
- All About the Base
- All About the Exponent
- Combining Exponential Expressions

EXPONENTS

The mathematical expression 4^3 consists of a base (4) and an exponent (3).

The expression is read as "four to the third power." The base (4) is multiplied by itself as many times as the power requires (3).

Thus $4^3 = 4 \times 4 \times 4 = 64$.

Two exponents have special names: the exponent 2 is called the square, and the exponent 3 is called the cube.

5^2 can be read as five to the second power, or as five squared ($5^2 = 5 \times 5 = 25$).
5^3 can be read as five to the third power, or as five cubed ($5^3 = 5 \times 5 \times 5 = 125$).

Just as multiplication is repeated addition, raising a number to a power is simply repeated multiplication.

Wow, That Increased Exponentially!

Have you ever heard the expression: "Wow, that increased exponentially!"? This phrase captures the essence of exponents. When a number (a positive number greater than 1) increases exponentially, it does not merely increase; it increases a whole lot in a short amount of time.

An important property of exponents is that the greater the exponent, the faster the rate of increase. Consider the following progression:

$5^1 = 5$
$5^2 = 25$ Increased by 20
$5^3 = 125$ Increased by 100
$5^4 = 625$ Increased by 500

The important thing to remember is that, for positive bases bigger than 1, the greater the exponent, the faster the rate of increase.

All About the Base

THE SIGN OF THE BASE

The base of an exponential expression may be either positive or negative. With a negative base, simply multiply the negative number as many times as the exponent requires.

For example:

$$(-4)^2 = (-4) \times (-4) = 16 \qquad (-4)^3 = (-4) \times (-4) \times (-4) = -64$$

Beware of even exponents on the GMAT. They hide the original sign of the base.

THE EVEN EXPONENT IS DANGEROUS: IT HIDES THE SIGN OF THE BASE!

One of the GMAT's most oft-used tricks involves the even exponent. In most cases, when an integer is raised to a power, the answer keeps the original sign of the base.

Examples:

$3^2 = 9$	$(-3)^3 = -27$	$3^3 = 27$
(positive base, positive answer)	(negative base, negative answer)	(positive base, positive answer)

However, any base raised to an even power will always result in a positive answer.

Examples:

$3^2 = 9$	$(-3)^2 = 9$	$(-3)^4 = 81$
(positive base, positive answer)	(negative base, positive answer)	(negative base, positive answer)

Therefore, when a base is raised to an even exponent, the resulting answer may either keep or change the original sign of the base. Whether $x = 3$ or -3, $x^2 = 9$. This makes even exponents extremely dangerous, especially in the hands of the GMAT test writers.

Consider this problem:

If $x^2 = 16$, is x equal to 4?

Your initial inclination is probably to say yes. However, x may not be 4; it may be -4! Thus, we cannot answer the question without additional information. Only if we are told that x is positive, can we answer affirmatively that x must be 4. Beware whenever you see an even exponent on the test.

Note that odd exponents are harmless, since they always keep the original sign of the base. For example, in the expression $x^3 = 64$, you can be sure that $x = 4$. You know that x is not -4 because $(-4)^3$ would yield -64.

A BASE OF 0 or 1
An exponential expression with a base of 0 always yields 0, regardless of the exponent.
An exponential expression with a base of 1 always yields 1, regardless of the exponent.

For example, $0^3 = 0 \times 0 \times 0 = 0$ and $0^4 = 0 \times 0 \times 0 \times 0 = 0$.
Similarly, $1^3 = 1 \times 1 \times 1 = 1$ and $1^4 = 1 \times 1 \times 1 \times 1 = 1$.

Thus, if you are told that $x^6 = x^7 = x^{15}$, you know that x must be either 0 or 1.

Of course, if you are told that $x^6 = x^8 = x^{10}$, x could be 0, 1 *or* −1. (See why even exponents are so dangerous?)

A FRACTIONAL BASE
When the base of an exponential expression is a fraction between 0 and 1, an interesting thing occurs: as the exponent increases, the value of the expression decreases!

> Combine successive exponents by multiplying the powers.

$$\left(\frac{3}{4}\right)^1 = \frac{3}{4} \qquad \left(\frac{3}{4}\right)^2 = \left(\frac{3}{4}\right) \times \left(\frac{3}{4}\right) = \frac{9}{16} \qquad \left(\frac{3}{4}\right)^3 = \left(\frac{3}{4}\right) \times \left(\frac{3}{4}\right) \times \left(\frac{3}{4}\right) = \frac{27}{64}$$

See that $\dfrac{3}{4} > \dfrac{9}{16} > \dfrac{27}{64}$. Powers operate as decreasing mechanisms on positive fractions.

All About the Exponent

THE SIGN OF THE EXPONENT

An exponent is not always positive. What happens if the exponent is negative?

$$5^{-1} = \frac{1}{5^1} = \frac{1}{5} \qquad 4^{-2} = \frac{1}{4^2} = \frac{1}{4 \times 4} = \frac{1}{16} \qquad (-2)^{-3} = \frac{1}{(-2)^3} = -\frac{1}{8}$$

Notice that an expression with a negative exponent yields the reciprocal of that expression with a positive exponent. When you see a negative exponent, think reciprocal!

AN EXPONENT OF 0 or 1

Any base raised to the exponent of 1 keeps the original base. This is obvious and true.

$$3^1 = 3 \qquad 4^1 = 4 \qquad (-6)^1 = -6 \qquad \left(-\frac{1}{2}\right)^1 = -\frac{1}{2}$$

By definition, any base raised to the 0 power yields 1. This is not intuitive but it is true.

$$3^0 = 1 \qquad 4^0 = 1 \qquad (-6)^0 = 1 \qquad \left(-\frac{1}{2}\right)^0 = 1$$

> When raising a power to a power, combine exponents by multiplying.

SUCCESSIVE EXPONENTS

A base raised to successive exponents means a base raised to one exponent and then that value raised to another exponent.

For example: $\left(3^2\right)^4$ Here, the base 3 is first squared, and then the result (which is 9) is raised to the fourth power.

However, there is a rule for combining successive exponents that can make the computation much easier and faster. Look at what happens when we write out each step of the previous example without doing any computation:

$$
\begin{aligned}
\left(3^2\right)^4 &= (3^2)(3^2)(3^2)(3^2) \\
&= (3 \times 3)(3 \times 3)(3 \times 3)(3 \times 3) \\
&= 3 \times 3 \times 3 \times 3 \times 3 \times 3 \times 3 \times 3 = 3^8 \\
&= (3)^{2 \times 4}
\end{aligned}
$$

Rule: When raising a power to a power, combine exponents by multiplying.

Combining Exponential Expressions

Now that you have the basics down for working with bases and exponents, what about working with more than one exponential expression at a time? If two exponential expressions have a base in common or an exponent in common, you can combine them.

WHEN CAN YOU COMBINE THEM?

(1)   You can only combine exponential expressions that are linked by multiplication or division. You can NEVER combine expressions linked by addition or subtraction.

(2)   You can combine exponential expressions if they have either a base or an exponent in common.

HOW CAN YOU COMBINE THEM?

If you forget these rules, you can derive them on the test by writing out the exponential expressions, as we did above.

The GMAT will often try to trick you into adding or subtracting exponential expressions that have a base or an exponent in common. Remember that you can only simplify when multiplying or dividing exponential expressions!

	SAME BASE	SAME EXPONENT
MULTIPLY	When multiplying expressions with the same base, ADD the exponents first. $(3^2)(3^3) = (3)(3)(3)(3)(3) = 3^5$	When multiplying expressions with the same exponent, MULTIPLY the bases first. $(3^3)(5^3) = (3)(3)(3)(5)(5)(5)$ $= (15)(15)(15) = 15^3$
DIVIDE	When dividing expressions with the same base, SUBTRACT the exponents first. $\dfrac{3^5}{3^2} = \dfrac{(3)(3)(3)(3)(3)}{(3)(3)}$ $= (3)(3)(3) = 3^3$	When dividing expressions with the same exponent, DIVIDE the bases first. $\dfrac{9^3}{3^3} = \dfrac{(9)(9)(9)}{(3)(3)(3)} = (3)(3)(3) = 3^3$

These expressions CAN'T be simplified:

$$7^4 + 7^6$$

$$3^4 + 12^4$$

$$6^5 - 6^3$$

$$12^7 - 3^7$$

These expressions CAN be simplified:

$$(7^4)(7^6)$$

$$(3^4)(12^4)$$

$$\frac{6^5}{6^3}$$

$$\frac{12^7}{3^7}$$

Try using the rules outlined above to simplify the expressions in the right column.

If the bases are the same, add or subtract the exponents. If the exponents are the same, multiply or divide the bases.

Problem Set

Simplify and solve the following problems using the rules for exponents.

1. 2^{-5}

2. $\dfrac{7^6}{7^4}$

3. $8^4(5^4)$

4. $2^4 \times 2^5 \div 2^7 - 2^4$

5. $\dfrac{9^4}{3^4} + \left(4^2\right)^3$

6. Does $a^2 + a^4 = a^6$ for all values of a?

7. If $x^3 = x^{15}$, and $x > 0$, what is x?

8. $x^3 < x^2$. Give three possible values for x.

9. If $x^4 = 16$, what is $|x|$?

10. If $y^5 > 0$, is $y < 0$?

11. If $b > a > 0$, and $c \neq 0$, is $a^2 b^3 c^4$ positive?

12. Simplify: $\dfrac{y^2 \times y^5}{(y^2)^4}$

13. If $r^3 + |r| = 0$, what are the possible values of r?

14. If $a^2 = 64$ and $b^4 = 1$, what are all the possible values of ab?

15. Simplify: $\dfrac{m^8 p^7 r^{12}}{m^3 r^9 p} \times p^2 r^3 m^4$

1. **1/32:** Remember that a negative exponent yields the reciprocal of the same expression with a positive exponent. $2^{-5} = \dfrac{1}{2^5} = \dfrac{1}{32}$

2. **49:** $\dfrac{7^6}{7^4} = 7^{6-4} = 7^2 = 49$

3. **2,560,000:** $8^4(5^4) = 40^4 = 2,560,000$

4. **−12:** $\dfrac{2^4 \times 2^5}{2^7} - 2^4 = 2^{(4+5-7)} - 2^4 = 2^2 - 2^4 = 4 - 16 = -12.$

5. **4177:** $\dfrac{9^4}{3^4} + \left(4^2\right)^3 = 3^4 + 4^6 = 81 + 4096 = 4177.$

6. **NO:** Remember, you cannot combine exponential expressions linked by addition.

7. **1:** If $x^3 = x^{15}$, x could be -1, 0, or 1. Given the additional fact that $x > 0$, x can only be 1.

8. **Any non-zero number less than 1:** As positive proper fractions are multiplied, their value decreases. For example, $(1/2)^3 < (1/2)^2$. Also, any negative number will make this inequality true. A negative number cubed is negative. Any negative number squared is positive. For example, $(-3)^3 < (-3)^2$.

9. **2:** The possible values for x are 2 and -2. The absolute value of both 2 and -2 is 2.

10. **NO:** An integer raised to an odd exponent retains the original sign of the base. Therefore, if y^5 is positive, y is positive.

11. **YES:** b and a are both positive numbers. Whether c is positive or negative, c^4 is positive. (Recall that any number raised to an even power is positive.) Therefore, the product $a^2b^3c^4$ is the product of 3 positive numbers, which will be positive.

12. $\dfrac{\mathbf{1}}{\mathbf{y}}$: $\dfrac{y^2 \times y^5}{(y^2)^4} = \dfrac{y^7}{y^8} = y^{7-8} = y^{-1} = \dfrac{1}{y}$

13. **0, −1:** If $r^3 + \left|r\right| = 0$, then r^3 must be the opposite of $\left|r\right|$. The only values for which this would be true are 0, which is the opposite of itself, and -1, whose opposite is 1.

14. **8 and −8:** If $a^2 = 64$, a can be either 8 or -8. If $b^4 = 1$, b can be either 1 or -1. Therefore, the product ab can be equal to either 8 or -8.

15. $\boldsymbol{m^9p^8r^6}$: $\dfrac{m^8p^7r^{12}}{m^3r^9p} \times p^2r^3m^4 = \dfrac{m^{12}p^9r^{15}}{m^3r^9p} = m^{(12-3)}p^{(9-1)}r^{(15-9)} = m^9p^8r^6$

g

Chapter 6

of

NUMBER PROPERTIES

ROOTS

In This Chapter . . .

- A Square Root Has Only One Answer
- Simplifying a Root
- Imperfect vs. Perfect Squares
- Simplifying an Imperfect Square
- Memorize: Squares and Square Roots
- Memorize: Cubes and Cube Roots

ROOTS

A root (also called a radical) is, in some sense, the opposite of an exponent.

$\sqrt[3]{64}$ is an expression that means: What number, when multiplied by itself three times, will yield 64?

The answer is 4, because $4 \times 4 \times 4 = 64$. Thus $\sqrt[3]{64} = 4$. We can say that 4 is the cube root of 64.

The most common type of root is a square root: $\sqrt{64}$. Notice that a square root is so common that it is written without the small 2 on the outside of the radical symbol. The expression $\sqrt{64}$ means: What number, when multiplied by itself, will yield 64? The answer is 8, because $8 \times 8 = 64$. Thus, the square root of 64 is 8.

Since square roots have only one solution, they are less tricky and dangerous than even exponents.

A Square Root Has Only One Value

Unlike even exponents, which yield both a positive and a negative solution, square roots have only one solution. For example:

   If $\sqrt{4}$ = x, what is x?

In the above example, $x = 2$, since $(2)(2) = 4$. While it is true that $(-2)(-2) = 4$, the GMAT follows the standard convention that a radical (root) sign denotes only the non-negative root of a number. Thus, 2 is the only solution for x.

Simplifying a Root

Sometimes there are two numbers inside the radical sign. In order to simplify this type of root, it is often helpful to split up the numbers into two roots and then solve. Other times, the opposite is true: there are two roots which you would like to simplify by combining them under one radical sign.

<u>WHEN CAN YOU COMBINE THEM?</u>
You can only combine roots in multiplication and division. You can NEVER combine roots in addition or subtraction.

<u>HOW CAN YOU COMBINE THEM?</u>
When multiplying roots, you can split up a larger product into its separate factors. Creating two radicals and solving each individually before multiplying can save you from long computation. Similarly, you can also combine two roots that are being multiplied together into a single root of the product.

> EX. $\sqrt{25 \times 16} = \sqrt{25} \times \sqrt{16} = 5 \times 4 = 20$
> $\sqrt{25} \times \sqrt{16} = \sqrt{25 \times 16} = \sqrt{400} = 20$

Dividing roots works the same way. You can split a larger quotient into the dividend and divisor. You can also combine two roots that are being divided into a single root of the quotient.

> EX. $\sqrt{144 \div 16} = \sqrt{144} \div \sqrt{16} = 12 \div 4 = 3$
> $\sqrt{144} \div \sqrt{16} = \sqrt{144 \div 16} = \sqrt{9} = 3$

The GMAT will often try to trick you into splitting the sum or difference of two numbers inside a radical into two individual roots. Or they will trick you into combining the sum or difference of two roots inside one radical sign. **Remember that you may only split or combine the <u>product</u> or <u>quotient</u> of two roots.**

> **WRONG:** $\sqrt{16 + 9} = \sqrt{16} + \sqrt{9} = 4 + 3 = 7$
> CORRECT: $\sqrt{16 + 9} = \sqrt{25} = 5$

You can NEVER combine roots in addition or subtraction. Only combine roots in multiplication and division.

Imperfect vs. Perfect Squares

Not all square roots yield an integer. For example: $\sqrt{52}$ does not yield an integer answer because no integer multiplied by itself will yield 52. $\sqrt{52}$ is an example of an imperfect square because it does not yield an integer answer.

$\sqrt{52}$ is between what two integers?

Find the closest square roots that you do know. We know that $\sqrt{49} = 7$ and $\sqrt{64} = 8$. Thus we can estimate that $\sqrt{52}$ is between 7 and 8. A good estimate might be 7.2. (Notice that we estimated the number to be closer to 7 than to 8, because $\sqrt{52}$ is closer to $\sqrt{49}$ than it is to $\sqrt{64}$.)

Simplifying an Imperfect Square

If we do not want to estimate an imperfect square such as $\sqrt{52}$, there is a more accurate method of simplifying it. Simply rewrite $\sqrt{52}$ as a product of primes inside the radical.

$$\sqrt{52} = \sqrt{2 \times 2 \times 13}$$

We can simplify any pairs inside the radical. In this case, there is a pair of 2's. Since $\sqrt{2 \times 2} = \sqrt{4} = 2$, we can rewrite $\sqrt{52}$ as follows:

$$\sqrt{52} = \sqrt{2 \times 2 \times 13} = 2 \times \sqrt{13}$$

This is often written as $2\sqrt{13}$. Let's look at another example:

Find $\sqrt{72}$.

We can rewrite $\sqrt{72}$ as a product of primes: $\sqrt{72} = \sqrt{2 \times 2 \times 2 \times 3 \times 3}$. Since there are a pair of 2's and a pair of 3's inside the radical, we can simplify them. We are left with: $\sqrt{72} = 2 \times 3 \times \sqrt{2} = 6\sqrt{2}$.

> 49 is an example of a perfect square because $\sqrt{49}$ does yield an integer. If $\sqrt{x}$ yields an integer, then we call x a perfect square (4, 9, 16, 25, etc.).

Memorize: Squares and Square Roots

You should memorize the following squares and square roots as they appear often on the GMAT.

$1^2 = 1$	$\sqrt{1} = 1$
$1.4^2 \approx 2$	$\sqrt{2} \approx 1.4$
$1.7^2 \approx 3$	$\sqrt{3} \approx 1.7$
$2^2 = 4$	$\sqrt{4} = 2$
$3^2 = 9$	$\sqrt{9} = 3$
$4^2 = 16$	$\sqrt{16} = 4$
$5^2 = 25$	$\sqrt{25} = 5$
$6^2 = 36$	$\sqrt{36} = 6$
$7^2 = 49$	$\sqrt{49} = 7$
$8^2 = 64$	$\sqrt{64} = 8$
$9^2 = 81$	$\sqrt{81} = 9$
$10^2 = 100$	$\sqrt{100} = 10$
$11^2 = 121$	$\sqrt{121} = 11$
$12^2 = 144$	$\sqrt{144} = 12$
$13^2 = 169$	$\sqrt{169} = 13$

Memorize these squares and cubes so you will recognize them quickly on the GMAT.

Memorize: Cubes and Cube Roots

You should memorize the following cubes and cube roots as they appear often on the GMAT.

$1^3 = 1$	$\sqrt[3]{1} = 1$
$2^3 = 8$	$\sqrt[3]{8} = 2$
$3^3 = 27$	$\sqrt[3]{27} = 3$
$4^3 = 64$	$\sqrt[3]{64} = 4$
$5^3 = 125$	$\sqrt[3]{125} = 5$

Problem Set

Solve or simplify the following problems using your rules for roots.

1. $\sqrt[3]{8}$

2. $\sqrt{18} \div \sqrt{2}$

3. $\sqrt{75}$

4. $\sqrt{63} + \sqrt{28}$

5. $\sqrt{20 \times 5}$

6. $\sqrt[3]{100 - 36}$

7.   Estimate $\sqrt{80}$ to the nearest tenth.

8. $\sqrt{20a} \times \sqrt{5a}$

9. $10\sqrt{12} \div 2\sqrt{3}$

10. $\sqrt[3]{-1}$

11. $\sqrt{150} - \sqrt{50}$

12. $\sqrt{x^4}$

13. $\sqrt{20(4) - 5(7)}$

14. $\sqrt{x^2y^3 + 3x^2y^3}$ (assume x is positive)

15. $\sqrt{.0081}$

1. **2:** The cube root of 8 is the number that, when multiplied by itself three times, yields 8.

2. **3:** $\sqrt{18} \div \sqrt{2} = \sqrt{9} = 3$

3. **5$\sqrt{3}$:** $\sqrt{75} = \sqrt{25} \times \sqrt{3} = 5\sqrt{3}$

4. **5$\sqrt{7}$:** $\sqrt{63} + \sqrt{28} = (\sqrt{9} \times \sqrt{7}) + (\sqrt{4} \times \sqrt{7}) = 3\sqrt{7} + 2\sqrt{7} = 5\sqrt{7}$

5. **10:** $\sqrt{20 \times 5} = \sqrt{100} = 10$

6. **4:** $\sqrt[3]{100 - 36} = \sqrt[3]{64} = 4$

7. **8.9:** 80 is in between two perfect squares: 64, which is 8^2, and 81, which is 9^2. Note that 80 is very close to 9^2. Therefore, a reasonable estimate for $\sqrt{80}$ is 8.9.

8. **10a:** $\sqrt{20a} \times \sqrt{5a} = \sqrt{100a^2} = 10a$

9. **10:** $10\sqrt{12} \div 2\sqrt{3} = \dfrac{10(\sqrt{4} \times \sqrt{3})}{2\sqrt{3}} = \dfrac{20\sqrt{3}}{2\sqrt{3}} = 10$

10. **-1:** $(-1)(-1)(-1) = -1$

11. **5$\sqrt{6}$ $-$ 5$\sqrt{2}$:** $\sqrt{150} - \sqrt{50} = (\sqrt{25} \times \sqrt{6}) - (\sqrt{25} \times \sqrt{2}) = 5\sqrt{6} - 5\sqrt{2}$

12. **x^2:** $\sqrt{x^4} = x^2$

13. **3$\sqrt{5}$:** $\sqrt{20(4) - 5(7)} = \sqrt{45} = \sqrt{9} \times \sqrt{5} = 3\sqrt{5}$

14. **2$xy\sqrt{y}$:** $\sqrt{x^2y^3 + 3x^2y^3} = \sqrt{4x^2y^3} = 2xy\sqrt{y}$ (since x is positive, $\sqrt{x^2} = x$)

15. **.09:** $(.09)(.09) = .0081$

g | Chapter 7
of

NUMBER PROPERTIES

PEMDAS

In This Chapter . . .

- PEMDAS: Order of Operations

A Note About PEMDAS

On the GMAT, you need to know the correct order of operations when simplifying an expression. The correct order of operations is: Parentheses-Exponents-Multiplication-Division-Addition-Subtraction.

$$5 + (2 \times 4 + 2)^2 - |7(-4)| + 18 \div 3 \times 5 - 8$$

P = PARENTHESES. First, perform all the operations that are INSIDE parentheses. Note that absolute value signs are taken as parentheses as well. In this expression, there are two groups of parentheses:

$$(2 \times 4 + 2) \text{ and } |7(-4)|$$

In the first group, there are two operations to perform, multiplication and addition. Using PEMDAS, we see that multiplication must come before addition.

$$(2 \times 4 + 2) = (8 + 2) = 10$$

In the second group, there is only one operation: multiplication. We do this and then we find the absolute value. Now our original expression looks like this:

$$|7(-4)| = |-28| = 28$$

$$5 + (10)^2 - 28 + 18 \div 3 \times 5 - 8$$

E = EXPONENTS. Second, take care of any exponents in the expression. Our expression only has one exponent. Now our expression looks like this:

$$(10)^2 = 100$$

$$5 + 100 - 28 + 18 \div 3 \times 5 - 8$$

M/D = MULTIPLICATION & DIVISION. Next, we perform all the multiplication and division. It is important to note that multiplication does NOT necessarily come before division. Instead, they should be performed in order from left to right. In our expression, you can see that the division must come first. Now our expression reads:

$$18 \div 3 \times 5$$

$$5 + 100 - 28 + 30 - 8$$

A/S = ADDITION & SUBTRACTION. Lastly, we perform all the addition and subtraction. It is important to note here again that addition does NOT necessarily come before subtraction. Instead, they should be performed in order from left to right.

$$5 + 100 - 28 + 30 - 8$$
$$105 - 28 + 30 - 8$$
$$77 + 30 - 8$$
$$107 - 8$$

Thus, after performing PEMDAS, we arrive at our answer: **99**

An easy way to remember this order is by the word PEMDAS. Or you can think of the phrase "Please Excuse My Dear Aunt Sally."

Chapter 8
of
NUMBER PROPERTIES

STRATEGIES FOR
DATA SUFFICIENCY

In This Chapter . . .

- Rephrasing
- Value vs. Yes/No Questions
- Testing Numbers
- Test Smart Numbers
- The Statements Never Contradict Each Other
- Sample Rephrasings for Challenging Problems

Rephrasing

Data sufficiency problems involve an element of disguise, in which the mathematical content and information are obscured in some way. Therefore, your first task in solving a data sufficiency problem is to rephrase the question and/or the statements whenever possible.

In problems that deal with number properties, you can often rephrase the question to incorporate familiar rules, such as the ones you have studied in this strategy guide. For example:

> **If p is an integer, is $\dfrac{p}{18}$ an integer?**
>
> (1) $\dfrac{5p}{18}$ is an integer.
>
> (2) $\dfrac{6p}{18}$ is an integer.

A Statement (1) ALONE is sufficient, but statement (2) alone is not sufficient.
B Statement (2) ALONE is sufficient, but statement (1) alone is not sufficient.
C BOTH statements TOGETHER are sufficient, but NEITHER statement ALONE is sufficient.
D EACH statement ALONE is sufficient.
E Statements (1) and (2) together are NOT sufficient.

If $\dfrac{p}{18}$ is an integer, this means that p is DIVISIBLE by 18.

The prime factorization of 18 is $3 \times 3 \times 2$. In order for the integer p to be divisible by 18, it must be divisible by two 3's and a 2. Using the prime box strategy explained earlier in this guide, we can rephrase the question as follows:

> **Are there two 3's and a 2 in p's prime box?**

Now, we can rephrase each statement.

Statement (1) can be restated as $5p$ is divisible by 18, or by two 3's and a 2. A double prime box, as shown to the right, allows you to separate the factors of a larger product.

Since we know that the two 3's and the 2 are not factors of 5, they must be put in p's prime box. Thus, statement (1) can be rephrased:

> **There are (at least) two 3's and a 2 in p's prime box.**

This is sufficient to answer the question.

Statement (2) can be restated as $6p$ is divisible by 18 or by two 3's and a 2. A double prime box, as shown to the right, allows you to separate the factors of a larger product.

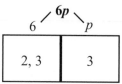

One 2 and one 3 are factors of 6. This only allows us to put one 3 in p's prime box. While there may be additional primes in p's prime box, statement (2) only *guarantees* one 3 in p's prime box. Thus, statement (2) can be rephrased as follows:

There is (at least) one 3 in p's prime box.

This is not sufficient to answer the question. Thus, the answer to this data sufficiency problem is (A): Statement (1) ALONE is sufficient, but statement (2) alone is not sufficient.

The preceding problem tests your knowledge of divisibility. However, the mathematical content being tested is disguised. Rephrasing allows you to remove that disguise and to demonstrate your knowledge of number properties. Let's look at another example:

If x is a positive integer, is $x^3 - 3x^2 + 2x$ divisible by 4?

(1) $x = 4y + 4$, where y is an integer
(2) $x = 2z + 2$, where z is an integer

Rephrase the question by factoring:

$$x^3 - 3x^2 + 2x = x(x^2 - 3x + 2) = x(x - 1)(x - 2)$$

This series represents three consecutive integers: $x - 2$, $x - 1$, and x. Therefore, the question is really asking:

Is the product of three consecutive integers, $x - 2$, $x - 1$, and x, divisible by 4?

One way that the product of 3 consecutive integers will be divisible by 4 is if 2 of those integers are even. For this to be the case in the product above, the first and last of the consecutive integers ($x - 2$ and x) must be even.

Thus, an even better rephrasing is:

Is x even?

Note: It is possible that x is not even and the product is still divisible by 4. This would be the case if the middle integer, $x - 1$, is a multiple of 4. Although the GMAT rarely tests this principle, we might incorporate it by adding a second possibility into our rephrased question as follows:

Is x even?   OR   Is $x - 1$ a multiple of 4?

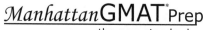

Now let's rephrase the statements.

Statement (1) tells us that $x = 4y + 4$, where y is an integer.

Since y is an integer, $4y$ must be a multiple of 4. Adding another 4 to a multiple of 4 means that the result will also be a multiple of 4. Thus, x is a multiple of 4, which means that x is even.

Statement (1) can be rephrased as follows: **x is even.** This is sufficient to answer our rephrased question.

Statement (2) tells us that $x = 2z + 2$, where z is an integer.

Since z is an integer, $2z$ must be a multiple of 2. Adding another 2 to a multiple of 2 means that the result will also be a multiple of 2. Thus, x is a multiple of 2, which means that x is even.

Statement (2) can be rephrased as follows: **x is even.** This is sufficient to answer our rephrased question.

Therefore, the answer to this data sufficiency problem is (D): EACH statement ALONE is sufficient.

> To rephrase a statement, take the given information, reduce it into its simplest form, and focus on how the piece of information relates to the question.

Types of Data Sufficiency Problems: Value vs. Yes/No

There are two types of data sufficiency problems:

(1) VALUE: These questions require you to solve for one numerical value:

What is the value of $x + y$?
How old is Vera?
In what year were the most rabbits born?

The information in the statements can be considered sufficient if it allows you to find a single number to answer the question. If the information yields more than one value, the information is insufficient.

(2) YES/NO: These questions require you to give a simple yes or no answer:

Is n divisible by 17?
Is $x + y$ prime?
Is $y < 0$?

The information in the statements can be considered sufficient if it allows you to conclusively answer YES or NO. If the answer is MAYBE, the information is insufficient.

Testing Numbers

Another strategy that is helpful for solving data sufficiency problems that deal with number properties is to test numbers—trying to find examples that yield multiple answers to a VALUE question and that make the answer to a YES/NO question MAYBE. If you can do this, you can conclude that the information you have is NOT SUFFICIENT. Here is an example:

If *n* is an integer and n^3 is between 1 and 100, inclusive, what is the value of *n*?

> **(1) *n* = 2*k* + 1, where *k* is an integer.**
> **(2) *n* is a prime number.**

In this problem, we are working with a small list of possibilities: integers whose cubes are between 1 and 100. The only integers that meet this criteria are 1, 2, 3, and 4, as shown in the box to the right. The simplest way to solve this problem is to use the information given in each statement to test this list. If the information eliminates all but one value, it is sufficient; if it yields multiple values, it is not sufficient.

$$1^3 = 1$$
$$2^3 = 8$$
$$3^3 = 27$$
$$4^3 = 64$$

Statement (1) tells us that *n* can be any odd number. The general expression for an even integer is 2*k*, where *k* is any integer; the general expression for an odd integer is 2*k* + 1. Therefore, of the four values on the list, *n* could be 1 or 3. Since statement (1) yields two possible values, it is NOT sufficient to answer the question.

Statement (2) tells us that *n* is a prime number, so *n* could be either 2 or 3. Statement (2) yields two possible values, so it is NOT sufficient either.

If we look at both statements together, *n* must be equal to 3, the intersection of the two statements. Statement (1) eliminates the possibility that *n* is the even number 2 or 4. Statement (2) eliminates the possibility that *n* is the non-prime number 1 or 4. We are left with only one value: *n* must be equal to 3.

The answer to this data sufficiency problem is (C): BOTH statements TOGETHER are sufficient, but NEITHER statement ALONE is sufficient.

You can test numbers to solve this example as well:

Is the positive integer *n* divisible by 108?

> **(1) *n* is divisible by 12.**
> **(2) *n* is a multiple of 9.**

Statement (1) tells us that *n* must be divisible by 12. This means that *n* could be 12, which is NOT divisible by 108, OR *n* could be 108, which IS divisible by 108. Statement (1) yields the answer MAYBE, which means it is not sufficient.

Statement (2) tells us that n must be divisible by 9. This means that n could be 9, which is NOT divisible by 108, OR n could be 108, which IS divisible by 108. Statement (2) yields the answer MAYBE, which means it is not sufficient.

Taking both statements together, n must be divisible by BOTH 12 and 9. This means that n could be 36, which is NOT divisible by 108, OR n could be 108, which IS divisible by 108. Both statements combined yield the answer MAYBE, which means they are not sufficient.

The answer to this data sufficiency problem is (E): Statements (1) and (2) TOGETHER are NOT sufficient.

Test Smart Numbers

When testing numbers, you should be trying to prove the statement insufficient. So, be sure to try fractions, negatives, and zero, unless you are told in the question that the variables represent only integers, only positive numbers, or only non-zero numbers.

When you are using a number-testing strategy, try your best to find numbers that yield multiple answers for a value question, or a MAYBE answer for a YES/NO question. If you can do this, you have proven the statement insufficient. If you cannot do this, it is likely (but not certain) that the statement is sufficient.

When you are testing numbers, try to find numbers that prove the given information is NOT sufficient.

The Statements Never Contradict Each Other

A final strategy is to use the fact that the two statements in a data sufficiency problem will never contradict each other.

If y and n are positive integers, is yn divisible by 7?

(1) $n^2 - 14n + 49 = 0$
(2) $n + 2$ is the first of three consecutive integers whose product is 990.

Statement (1) can be factored: $n^2 - 14n + 49 = (n - 7)(n - 7) = 0$, so $n = 7$. Since $n = 7$ and y is an integer, yn must be divisible by 7. Statement (1) is sufficient to answer the question: YES, yn is divisible by 7.

Statement (2) tells us that the product of $(n + 2)$, $(n + 3)$, and $(n + 4)$ is equal to 990. If we test numbers, we find that the three consecutive integers whose product is 990 are 9, 10, and 11. (The fact that 990 is close to 1000 should provide a hint that the three numbers should be close to 10.)

Now let's say that we *incorrectly* identify n as 9, the first of the three consecutive integers. If $n = 9$, then we do not know whether yn is divisible by 7. MAYBE it is (if y is divisible by 7) or MAYBE it is not (if y is not divisible by 7). We conclude that statement (2) is not sufficient to answer the question.

Thus, we would identify the answer to this data sufficiency question as (A): Statement (1) ALONE is sufficient, but statement (2) alone is not sufficient.

But wait! Take a look again at the information we derived from each statement. Statement (1) told us that $n = 7$, while statement (2) told us that $n = 9$. This is not possible because the two data sufficiency statements on the GMAT always provide TRUE information. The two statements cannot contradict each other.

Whenever you find that your two statements contradict each other, it means that you've made a mistake! What mistake did we make in the logic above?

Our mistake here was in statement (2). We forgot that $n + 2$ (not n) is the first of the three consecutive integers. Thus, $n + 2 = 9$, while $n = 7$. Now statement (2) no longer contradicts statement (1). Knowing that $n = 7$ means that yn must be divisible by 7. Thus, statement (2) IS in fact sufficient to answer the question.

Using the principle that the two data sufficiency statements cannot contradict each other, we caught our mistake. The correct answer is actually (D): EACH statement ALONE is sufficient.

Rephrasing: Challenge Short Set

At the very end of this book, you will find lists of NUMBER PROPERTIES problems that have appeared on past official GMAT exams. These lists reference problems from *The Official Guide for GMAT Review, 11th Edition* and *The Official Guide for GMAT Quantitative Review* (the questions contained therein are the property of The Graduate Management Admission Council, which is not affiliated in any way with Manhattan GMAT).

As you work through the Data Sufficiency problems listed at the end of this book, be sure to focus on *rephrasing*. If possible, try to *rephrase* each question into its simplest form *before* looking at the two statements. In order to rephrase, focus on figuring out the specific information that is absolutely necessary to answer the question. After rephrasing the question, you should also try to *rephrase* each of the two statements, if possible. Rephrase each statement by simplifying the given information into its most basic form.

In order to help you practice rephrasing, we have taken the most difficult Data Sufficiency problems on *The Official Guide* problem list (these are the problem numbers listed in the "Challenge Short Set" on page 93) and have provided you with our own sample rephrasings for each question and statement. In order to evaluate how effectively you are using the rephrasing strategy, you can compare your rephrased questions and statements to our own rephrasings that appear below. Questions and statements that are significantly rephrased appear in **bold**.

Rephrasings from *The Official Guide For GMAT Review, 11th Edition*

The questions and statements that appear below are only our *rephrasings*. The original questions and statements can be found by referencing the problem numbers below in the Data Sufficiency section of *The Official Guide for GMAT Review, 11th edition* (pages 278-290).

101.   **Is $p = 3$?**

    (1) $p > 2$

    (2) No meaningful rephrasing can be done here. However, we *can* conclude that p is not necessarily equal to 3.

118.   Since $150 = 2 \times 3 \times 5 \times 5$,
    Is n equal to the products of some or all of the numbers 1, 2, 3, 5, and 5?

    (1) $n < 7$

    (2) n is a prime number

125.   **Is s a factor of r?**

    (1) All factors of s are factors of r.
    1 and s (the only factors of s we know) are factors of r.

    (2) All prime factors of s are prime factors of r. (No meaningful rephrasing can be done here. You can test numbers to see that this information is not sufficient.)

126. $z^n = 1$
    No meaningful rephrasing can be done here. However, you should recognize that this statement will be true if (a) $n = 0$ or (b) $z = 1$ or (c) $z = -1$ and n is even.

    (1) $z = \{1, -1\}$

    (2) No meaningful rephrasing can be done here. You can test numbers to see that this information is not sufficient.

132.   **Does $n = 2$?**

    (1) n **is prime**

    (2) No meaningful rephrasing can be done here. You can test numbers to see that this information means that $n = 2$ and is therefore sufficient.

144.   Is $\dfrac{1}{10^n} < \dfrac{1}{100}$?

       Is $\dfrac{1}{10^n} < \dfrac{1}{10^2}$?

       Is $n > 2$?

       (1) $n > 2$

       (2) $(1/10)^n \times (1/10)^{-1} < 1/10$
            $(1/10)^n \times 10 < 1/10$
                $(1/10)^n < 1/100$
                   $1/10^n < 1/10^2$
                     $n > 2$

147.   Is the product of consecutive integers $(n + 1)n(n - 1)$ divisible by 4?
       OR: Are there 2 even integers in the set of consecutive integers $(n + 1)$, n, $(n - 1)$?
       OR: (Best) **Is n odd?**

       (1) n is an even number plus 1
          n is odd

       (2) $n(n + 1)$ is divisible by 6.
          Either n OR $n + 1$ is even.

148.   What is the tens digit of positive integer x?
       No meaningful rephrasing can be done to the question.

       (1) $x = 100m + 30$ where m is a nonnegative integer

       (2) $x = 110n + 30$ where n is a nonnegative integer

149.   **Are x and y different (one even and one odd)?**

       (1) x and z are the same (either both even or both odd)

       (2) y and z are different (one even and one odd)

Rephrasings from *The Official Guide for GMAT Quantitative Review*

The questions and statements that appear below are only our *rephrasings*. The original questions and statements can be found by referencing the problem numbers below in the Data Sufficiency section of *The Official Guide for GMAT Quantitative Review* (pages 149-157).

3.   **How many factors does *n* have?**

   (1)   *n*

   $$\boxed{p, q}$$

   n has only 2 factors other than 1 and *n*: *p* and *q*.
   Since *p* and *q* are prime, there are no other factors.
   Thus, ***n* has 4 factors**.

   (2)   *n* has the same number of factors as 8; thus, ***n* has 4 factors**.

45.   **If *p* × *q* = 24, what number is *p*?**

   (1) *q* is divisible by 6; thus, *q* equals 24, 12, or 6. **p = 1, 2, or 4.**

   (2) *p* is divisible by 2 (OR, *p* is even). **p = 2, 4, 6, 8, 12, or 24.**

p	q
1	24
2	12
3	8
4	6
6	4
8	3
12	2
24	1

53.   **What is the value of x^{p-q}?**

   (1) $p - q = 0$

   (2) $x = 3$

63.   **Is *y* divisible by 3?**

   (1)   *y*

   $$\boxed{\begin{array}{c} 2 \\ 2 \end{array}}$$

   (2)   *y*

   $$\boxed{\begin{array}{c} 2 \\ 3 \end{array}}$$

75.   **Is p odd?**

(1) p is odd.

(2) **p is odd.**

78.   **Is x a positive proper fraction (a fraction between zero and one)?**

(1) $x < -1$ OR $x > 1$
x is NOT a positive proper fraction.

(2) $x > -1$
x MAY or MAY NOT be a positive proper fraction.

82.   **Is $m = n + 1$?**

(1) $m - 1 = (n + 1) + 1$ OR $m - 1 = (n + 1) - 1$
$m - 1 = n + 2$ $m - 1 = n$
$m = n + 3$ $m = n + 1$

Note that $m = n + 3$ contradicts the original question, and is therefore impossible. Discard this possibility. Thus, **$m = n + 1$**.

(2) m is divisible by 2.

83.   **Is n divisible by 7?**

(1) $n = 2k + 3$

(2) $2k - 4 = 7x$, where x is an integer

86.   There is little rephrasing you can do in this problem. Testing numbers is the best strategy.

108.   **Is d a perfect square?**

(1) d is a perfect square.

(2) $\sqrt{d}$ is a perfect square; therefore, **d is a perfect square**.

110.   **Are there three 2's and one 3 in the prime box for _n_?**

(1) **There are at least two 2's in the prime box.**

(2) **There is at least one 2 and at least one 3 in the prime box.**

111.   There is little rephrasing you can do in this problem. Testing numbers is the best strategy.

116.   **Is _x_ a perfect square?**

(1) $2\sqrt{x}$ is an integer
Therefore, _x_ **is a perfect square.**

(2) $\sqrt{3x}$ is not an integer.

Chapter 9
of
NUMBER PROPERTIES

OFFICIAL GUIDE
PROBLEM SETS

In This Chapter . . .

- Number Properties Problem Solving List
  from *The Official Guides*
- Number Properties Data Sufficiency List
  from *The Official Guides*

Practicing with REAL GMAT Problems

Now that you have completed your study of NUMBER PROPERTIES it is time to test your skills on problems that have actually appeared on real GMAT exams over the past several years.

The problem sets that follow are composed of questions from two books published by the Graduate Management Admission Council® (the organization that develops the official GMAT exam):

The Official Guide for GMAT Review, 11th Edition &
The Official Guide for GMAT Quantitative Review

These two books contain quantitative questions that have appeared on past official GMAT exams. (The questions contained therein are the property of The Graduate Management Admission Council, which is not affiliated in any way with Manhattan GMAT.)

Although the questions in the Official Guides have been "retired" (they will not appear on future official GMAT exams), they are great practice questions.

In order to help you practice effectively, we have categorized every problem in The Official Guides by topic and subtopic. On the following pages, you will find two categorized lists:

(1) **Problem Solving:** Lists all Problem Solving NUMBER PROPERTIES questions contained in *The Official Guides* and categorizes them by subtopic.

(2) **Data Sufficiency:** Lists all Data Sufficiency NUMBER PROPERTIES questions contained in *The Official Guides* and categorizes them by subtopic.

Note: Each book in Manhattan GMAT's 8-book preparation series contains its own *Official Guide* lists that pertain to the specific topic of that particular book. If you complete all the practice problems contained on the *Official Guide* lists in the back of each of the 8 Manhattan GMAT preparation books, you will have completed every single question published in *The Official Guides*. At that point, you should be ready to take your Official GMAT exam!

Problem Solving

from *The Official Guide for GMAT Review, 11th edition* (pages 20-23 & 152-186) and *The Official Guide for GMAT Quantitative Review* (pages 62-85)

<u>Note</u>: Problem numbers preceded by "D" refer to questions in the Diagnostic Test chapter of *The Official Guide for GMAT Review, 11th edition* (pages 20-23).

Solve each of the following problems in a notebook, making sure to demonstrate how you arrived at each answer by showing all of your work and computations. If you get stuck on a problem, look back at the NUMBER PROPERTIES strategies and content contained in this guide to assist you.

CHALLENGE SHORT SET

This set contains the more difficult number properties problems from each of the content areas.

> *11th edition*: D13, 33, 86, 114, 137, 159, 201, 204, 213, 233, 234, 236, 241, 249
> *Quantitative Review*: 103, 117, 122, 125, 145, 147, 149, 152, 160, 169, 170

FULL PROBLEM SET
Divisibility & Primes

> *11th edition*: D13, D15, D18, D23, 2, 5, 21, 33, 37, 71, 114, 148, 159, 207, 209, 213, 234, 241, 249
> *Quantitative Review*: 98, 102, 103, 109, 122, 125, 164, 169

Exponents & Roots

> *11th edition*: D17, 9, 29, 43, 49, 56, 57, 137, 233
> *Quantitative Review*: 34, 45, 64, 81, 97, 117, 145, 147, 149, 152, 163, 170

Odds & Evens

> *11th edition*: 108, 187
> *Quantitative Review*: 150

Positives & Negatives

> *11th edition*: 20, 26, 81
> *Quantitative Review*: 15, 53

Consecutive Integers

> *11th edition*: D2, 86, 201, 204, 215, 236, 242
> *Quantitative Review*: 9, 160

Data Sufficiency

from *The Official Guide for GMAT Review, 11th edition* (pages 24-25 & 278-290) and *The Official Guide for GMAT Quantitative Review* (pages 149-157)

Note: Problem numbers preceded by "D" refer to questions in the Diagnostic Test chapter of *The Official Guide for GMAT Review, 11th edition* (pages 24-25).

Solve each of the following problems in a notebook, making sure to demonstrate how you arrived at each answer by showing all of your work and computations. If you get stuck on a problem, look back at the NUMBER PROPERTIES strategies and content contained in this guide to assist you.

Practice REPHRASING both the questions and the statements. The majority of data sufficiency problems can be rephrased; however, if you have difficulty rephrasing a problem, try testing numbers to solve it.

It is especially important that you familiarize yourself with the directions for data sufficiency problems, and that you memorize the 5 fixed answer choices that accompany all data sufficiency problems.

CHALLENGE SHORT SET
This set contains the more difficult number properties problems from each of the content areas.
> *11th edition*: 101, 118, 125, 126, 132, 144, 147, 148, 149
> *Quantitative Review*: 3, 45, 53, 63, 75, 78, 82, 83, 86, 108, 110, 111, 116

FULL PROBLEM SET
Divisibility & Primes
> *11th edition*: D26, D42, 14, 22, 28, 101, 103, 118, 125, 132, 148, 153
> *Quantitative Review*: 3, 7, 13, 16, 33, 39, 45, 63, 83, 86, 88, 100, 110

Exponents & Roots
> *11th edition*: D44, 5, 126, 144, 146
> *Quantitative Review*: 18, 53, 73, 78, 98, 106, 108, 116

Odds & Evens
> *11th edition*: 17, 25, 65, 149
> *Quantitative Review*: 75

Positives & Negatives
> *11th edition*: D41, 135
> *Quantitative Review*: 76, 94, 101, 111

Consecutive Integers
> *11th edition*: 61, 83, 147
> *Quantitative Review*: 20, 82

To waive "Finance I" at Harvard Business School you must:
- (A) Be a CFA
- (B) Have prior coursework in finance
- (C) Have two years of relevant work experience in the financial sector
- (D) Pass a waiver exam
- (E) None of the above; one cannot waive core courses at HBS

What are the requirements of an Entrepreneurial Management major at the Wharton School?
- (1) Completion of 5 credit units (cu) that qualify for the major
- (2) Participation in the Wharton Business Plan Competition during the 2nd year of the MBA program

- (A) Statement (1) ALONE is sufficient, but statement (2) alone is not sufficient.
- (B) Statement (2) ALONE is sufficient, but statement (1) alone is not sufficient.
- (C) BOTH statements TOGETHER are sufficient, but NEITHER statement ALONE is sufficient.
- (D) EACH statement ALONE is sufficient.
- (E) Statements (1) and (2) TOGETHER are NOT sufficient.